AMERICA

The Chosen Nation

AMAKA OJIRIKA-NZERIBE

AMERICA The Chosen Nation

Quantity sales special discounts are available on quantity purchases by corporations, associations, and others. For details, contact the publisher at the address above.

The author and the editor have tried to recreate events, locales, and conversations from the author's memories of them. In order to maintain their anonymity and to protect the privacy of individuals in several instances the names of individuals and places were changed as well as some identifying characteristics and details such as physical properties, occupations, and places of residence. Any resemblance to actual living persons is purely coincidental.

Orders by U.S. trade bookstores and wholesalers. Email info@BeyondPublishing.net

The Beyond Publishing Speakers Bureau can bring authors to your live event. For more information or to book an event contact the Beyond Publishing Speakers Bureau speak@BeyondPublishing.net

The Author can be reached directly at BeyondPublishing.net

Manufactured and printed in the United States of America distributed globally by BeyondPublishing.net

New York | Los Angeles | London | Sydney

ISBN Hardcover: 978-1-637920-03-9

ISBN Softcover: 978-1-637920-18-3

AMERICA

The Chosen Nation

America is a great country. I'm very lucky to be blessed by the Almighty God, himself. I remember growing up in Africa that I always wished I would come to America. On December 25th, 1999, my dreams came true. I landed in the United States of America, in Dallas, Texas. That was the happiest day of my life. The first thing I noticed was that there was so much food everywhere. I was shocked. I started crying, because I remembered what we had gone through in Africa just to survive. We had to go to the stream twice a day, every day, to fetch water, and we had to carry it back home on our heads before we could cook. I wished I could carry some of the foods back to my friends. I was actually in awe that there was light every day and running water around the clock. I knew that this great move had been chosen by God, and He has blessed us so much. I couldn't believe that my dreams had come true. I said to myself, "You are actually in the United States. No more suffering. You can now be who you want to be." I couldn't sleep for so many nights, because I was so excited about everything. I said to myself, "Now, I have the privilege to better my life. I wouldn't have had this kind of opportunity if I was still back in Africa."

Psalms 33:12 reads, "Blessed are the nations whose God is the Lord, the people whom He has chosen for His own inheritance." Our Creator has certainly blessed America in tremendous ways, like the abundant, natural beauty that can be found all across our land— including tropical beaches, green valleys, rich farmlands, towering mountains, and more.

Now, let's talk about where we are today with Christ, and what went wrong. How can we allow the devil and his agents to destroy us, destroy this great country, and cause us to hate each other, fight each other, and disrespect each other? We have become so selfish and self-centered. Not being our brother's keeper. The devil is a big liar, but we can come back to God again and shame the devil. We have a Godly heritage. Fifty-two of our original founding fathers, who wrote our constitution, were Christians, and they established our country on Judeo-Christian values.

AMERICAS RESOURCES

Our land is blessed with plentiful, natural resources, including water, oil, and fertile farmland. We enjoy the liberty to speak our minds, worship as we choose, and live undisturbed, private lives. America's free-enterprise system allows almost anyone the opportunity to rise from poverty to wealth. Compared to most nations in the world, the United States has a high standard of living.

Our spiritual heritage is strong; we have been blessed with intellectual, spiritual giants—such as Jonathan Edwards, George Whitfield, and Charles Finney. Why would God bless America as He has? I believe the reason is He intends for us to be a role model to the world. Not only are we an example of liberty and democracy, but we also have the manpower to take the Gospel around the world. The United States of America has done just that, but what about the country as a whole?

Sadly, we have taken God's hand of blessing for granted—declining to bless Him, in return. We have also removed many things about God in our country, like:

1. Removing prayers and the Word of God from our schools. And we wonder why our kids don't have respect anymore… it is because we are not teaching them to fear God.

2. Allowed sex and violence to dominate our entertainment industry. People are selling their souls to the devil, just to be famous and rich.

3. Exported pornography to the world.

4. Legalized the murder of our unborn children. Those innocent voices are crying out for justice.

5. Lived reckless and undisciplined lives and satisfied our desires in unrighteous ways. We call that freedom.

We, as a nation, must go back to what our founders believed in, and because of that, America has been blessed.

"Do not be deceived. God is not to be mocked. For whatever a man sows, this he will also reap."—Galatians 6:7

This principle also applies to us— that we will reap what we sow. We may not currently be harvesting all the consequences of our rebellion, but that doesn't mean our nation will never be called to judgment. The Lord has chosen to bless us in the past, but that is no guarantee He will continue to do so.

"I might speak on concerning a nation, or concerning a Kingdom, to build up or to plant it; if it does evil in my sight by not obeying my voice, then I will think better of the good with which I have promised to bless it." –Jeremiah 18:9-10

Our country can not continue this current path without reaping God's judgment. Unless something changes, and changes fast, our future generations will not experience the freedom, prosperity, nor opportunity that you and I enjoy today— as followers of Christ. We have the responsibility to live holy lives, so you and I must speak out against indecencies, immoralities, and unrighteous laws. We should participate in electing and supporting Godly leaders. America needs God to heal again. Citizens need to know about the freedom and forgiveness Christ offers to all who surrender their lives to Him.

There is still time for our nation to repent and turn back to the Lord. He can sweep away the corruption in America, turn our country around, and use her powerfully to make a global impacts for His name. Will you be a part of this transformation?

Let's talk about the events of 2020: the year nobody will ever forget. God has actually shown the whole world that He is God—all by himself. He does not need our permission to be God. He also doesn't need our opinions for Him to be God. COVID-19 has taken the lives of over 200,000 Americans and put many more out of work. During quarantine, many of us have grown lonely and spiritually numb.

We, as human beings, worship everything, but God especially. We, as a nation, are consumed by our work, our celebrities, our money, our material things. We have shifted our focus to what is not important, rather than what is— which is God and His blessings upon our lives. Don't get me wrong; good things are good, but have you made time out of your busy schedule and recognized the one who made all that possible? How many times have you woken up in the morning and said, "God, thank you for waking me up today"?

The murder of George Floyd prompted our nation to reckon with our legacy of systemic racism, sparking protests and demands for justice. It seems like both our society and our personal lives are spiraling out of control.

Despite this personal and cultural exile, the Lord is not silent. What is God inviting us to in this upheaval? To answer that question, we will turn to Prophet Jeremiah, whose messages from God to his people contain vibrant and startling images that both expose our spiritual condition and magnify God's merciful heart toward us. We will see that God wants us back, and His offering to us is fresh hope, a clarified purpose, and a season of renewal.

2020—The wakeup call events of why God is shaking America and the world. God told us what He was going to do that would shake us: "Thus says the Lord of hosts once more, 'In a little while, I am going to shake the heaven and the Earth, the sea also, and the dry land. I will overthrow the throne of kingdoms and destroy the power of the kingdoms of the nations." –Haggai 2:6-7

This prophecy is an intercept from the mind of the all knowing, all-seeing God of the Universe.

Do you remember where you were on September 11th, 2001? Do you remember how you felt when you saw the Pentagon burning? The smoldering wreckage in Pennsylvania? The Twin Towers imploding? Not since Pearl Harbor had so many Americans been killed in a single attack, with more than 3,000 people dying that day. None of us will ever forget it. God allowed us to be shaken. The question remains: are we listening?

Nine of the ten most costly and expensive hurricanes in American history have happened since 9/11 .The worst was Hurricane Katrina, which nearly wiped out an entire American city and ended up costing 108 billion dollars.

Hurricane Irene likely ranks in the top five and made 2011 the worst year in American history for natural disasters— with ten, separate catastrophes costing 1-billion dollars or more.

At the same time, our economy is being shaken to its core, as 14 million Americans have lost their jobs just in the last few years. Millions of families have lost their homes. Washington is running up the national credit card to jumpstart our economy, but it is not working.

Clearly, there's a disconnect between who we say we are what we say we believe, and how we are living. How is this possible? How can we be salt and light to the lost world around us, if we are no different than it? How can possibly hope for a spiritual revival or a third Great Awakening in this land, if we always fighting each other? The devil is a liar. The gates of hell will not prevail over this great and mighty nation.

Luke 6:46 states, "Why do you call me, 'Lord, Lord,' and do not do what I say?" This is a very important question for our nation in this time when everything is going crazy.

Why is God shaking us?

The Bible teaches us that, at this stage in history, God is not shaking us to punish us. Though, judgment will come.

First, God is shaking us because He loves us, and He wants us to repent. 2 Chronicles 7:14 says, "If my People, which are called by my name, shall humble themselves, and pray, and seek my face, and turn from their wicked ways; then will I hear from heaven, and will forgive their sins, and will heal their land."

God is telling us to stop, because we are running in the opposite direction— away from Him. He's telling us to repent, to turn around, and to come running back to Him, so He can forgive us and dust us off and restore us. That's why He's shaking us. He is trying to get us to let go of everything and anything we are holding that is not Him in every form of ideology, physiology, religious belief, political belief, or material possession— whatever we are holding onto that we think will give us hope and peace and security other than Jesus Christ, His only begotten son.

Second, God is shaking us, because He wants us to realize there is no one else who can satisfy us or give us true peace and security, except Jesus Christ. There is no other water that will quench our spiritual and emotional thirst except His living water, and He wants us to discover Him and draw near to Him and drink the water only Jesus Christ can give us.

Third, God is shaking us, because He has a mission for His church— a mission for each follower of His good work that He prepared before the world began, and He doesn't want us to miss the blessing of serving Him and seeing Him bear fruit through our lives of obedience.

Is America trying to be Jonah? In the Bible, the Lord gave the Hebrew Prophet, Jonah, a mission to take a warning of judgment and of the urgency of repentance to the people of Nineveh—in modern-day, northern Iraq—but Jonah refused to listen to the word of the Lord and tried to run away by boarding a ship. The founders of this great country were fearful of God, and that's why God has blessed this nation so greatly. He wants for us to keep living in that very foundation, but we are trying to run, just like Jonah. We want our freedom so much more than wanting God. Who says that there is no freedom when you work and obey the laws given to us by God Almighty ? How convicting is this, that a pagan ship captain had to shake a teacher of God's Word and wake him up and beg him to pray for his salvation? What about America? What mission has God given us? Are we obeying, or are we on the run from the Lord and asleep to his voice of salvation?

There's a fourth reason, too: the Lord is shaking us because Jesus Christ is coming back soon, and the time for our nation to get right with the Lord is running out. How do we know Christ is coming back? Because He said so:

Revelation 22:12— "Jesus said, 'Behold, I am coming quickly, and my reward is with me to render every man according to what he has done.'"

John 14:1-6—"DO not let your hearts be troubled. Believe in God; believe also in me. In my father's house are many dwelling places; if it were not so, I would have told you, for I go to prepare a place for you. If I go and prepare a place for you, I will come again and receive you myself, that where I am there you may be also."

God has prepared a great place for us in this nation, only if we will turn to Him and bring Him back into this country, so we can have joy peace of the Almighty God. Then, our land shall be healed again.

In Matthew 24, Luke 21, Mark 13, and all throughout scripture, we find lists of signs:

1. Wars and rumors of war.

2. Uprisings and revolutions.

3. Earthquakes.

4. Natural disasters.

5. Lawlessness.

6. False prophets.

7. False teachers.

8. The rise of evil in our cultures.

9. Persecution of the believers.

10. Betrayals.

11. Immoralities.

These are just to name a few.

Jesus said that we will experience birth pangs. Are we not experiencing all these today? We are seeing the signs that will precede Christ's return. We are experiencing the chaos and hatred. We are being shaken, as the prophecy warned, because Jesus wants America to wake up.

Is America ready to see Jesus face-to-face? I don't think so. God is calling America back for a fresh start for righteous and willing spirits. To start, we need to wake up. COVID-19 came to wake us up, but it is very obvious that people have gone back to their evil ways once they went back to business as usual, and they completely missed the whole message of what God wanted us to start doing. God, please have mercy on us.

Let's be clear: the Bible tells us that these shakings are going to continue and get worse, increasing in frequency and intensity. Our Lord, Jesus Christ, is giving America time to rekindle our first love with Him, to embrace him back—especially in schools—to eat of the bread of life and stop murdering each other. To drink of the living water of love. To follow Him, as our founders did. To serve Him, no matter how high the cost is. To discover His mercies for America, which are fresh every day.

America is like Israel. It was established by God, Himself, and God gave Himself to the people by giving them the Ten Commandments and the Convenant. God only asked them for one thing in return, just like His asking America to love Him, obey Him, and serve Him. What did Israel do? They denied the Lord. They defied the law, and they defiled the land. So, God had to judge them, just like He did to America right now.

AMERICA HAS DENIED THE LORD

The Lord has slowly, but surely and steadily, been expelled from every public venue. It started in the public schools and has spread to our public places, our courthouses, our coins, our Pledge of Allegiance, and on and on— to the point we are fighting battles about what we can even say in the church. It is no longer just about the separation of Church and State, but rather, the separation of America from the God who founded and blessed her.

AMERICA HAS DEFIED THE LAW

The Supreme Court says that it is against the law to display the Ten Commandments in a public place by reasoning that if we display them, people might ponder and obey them. We are doing exactly what Israel did. It is now the official position of our government that the Ten Commandments are dangerous. Why wouldn't we want kids in school to see, "Thou shall not kill," if they obey it? The new direction our once-Christian nation is now going is just foolish and contrary to basic common sense. We don't force our beliefs on anyone, but we have allowed the world to chip away at our core of morality.

AMERICA HAS DEFILED THE LAND

We have done this in many ways, but perhaps the number-one way is found in the spilled blood of unborn babies. God took away His glory from Israel when they did such things, and I believe He is in the process of removing Himself from America. We need a national revival. We need a moral and spiritual awakening. I don't know what else is going to take to wake us up. When a family becomes rich, there are three stages which seem to always occur.

The first generation makes the fortune; the second generation speculate their fortune through a series of compromises and foolish decisions; and the third generation dissipates the fortune until it is gone. That is exactly how it works with a nation. There is a generation that spawns the freedom, and then, there is a generation that dissipates it until the freedom is no more. If you don't believe this, you need to study does nation the have forgotten God in history.

What do we know about the generation of Israel that entered into the Promised Land under the general, Joshua? Israel was given victory after victory by God, until the walls came tumbling down. Kings won victories they never could have apart from the power of God.

And that's just how America won the Revolutionary War. Britain had more men, more money, and better machinery. It was a truly a David and Goliath scenario— but God was on our side, and we won.

Patrick Henry said, "Is life so dear, or peace so sweet, as to be purchased at the price of chains or slavery? Forbid it, Almighty God! I know not what course others may take, but as for me, give me liberty or give me death!" It was game on, and we won that war. George Washington became our first president when he took office, and he placed his hand on the Holy Bible. His first official act was to lead the entire Congress in a two-hour worship session. In one of his inaugural addresses, he said, "No people can be bound to acknowledge and adore the invisible hand which conducts the affairs of men more than the people of the United States." In plain English, he said it was God who got us this far, and we had better not forget it. Wow, it seems like we have, indeed, forgotten about our roots.

Our founding fathers made it abundantly clear that this land was founded on God and the Bible.

SPECULATION

Succeeding generations in Israel began to squander their blessings all away. God practically said, "Look at all I have done for

you: I delivered you from slavery, fed you with manna, guided you. Now, look at you – why have you done this?" It looks to me like God is asking why America has done this to Him? The Joshua generation saw the great works of God firsthand. Sadly, this means they failed to pass the values onto their children. This has happened in America since 1960, and look where we are today: Americans are brainwashed by humanism, situational ethics, and relativism. We do not understand our moral foundations and the spiritual principles upon which this nation was founded. We are trying to rewrite history and remove God from our land. Judges 21:25 states, "In those days, there was no king in Israel. Every man did that which was right in his own eyes."

They became a people with no absolutes, no standard to live by. Is that not the nation you and I live in today? It is time we stop saying "look at what we can gain" and start asking "what might we lose by continuing this way?" Now, we are turning to burrowing and borrowing, not just from banks, but from China, especially.

DISSIPATES

On 9/11, terrorists turned planes into missiles The next day, Dr. Jerry Falwell said, "We'd better realize that God is removing His protection hand from this nation." Then, he specifically cited our nation's sins of abortion and homosexuality. Do you realize that Revelations describes the downfall of a world power like America, and that economic disaster might be us?

Some arrogantly question if a loving God would allow that? If we ask for it. Where was God when those students were gunned down by their classmates at Columbine? I will tell you where He was: America expelled Him in 1962. America threw out the Bible and prayer and said, "God, you are not welcome." And now, we are in a new generation. Could this be the final generation in America? Our forefathers generated so much. Are we the generation that will dissipate their work until it is completely gone? We are one generation away from losing our country. This new series will continue through Judges by looking at the judgment we have been asking for.

Is there any hope? Where there is God, there's still hope! That's why America needs God so badly right now— to heal this land. God would always rather forgive than judge. If we insist on turning on God, we should be afraid. After all God has done for America, how can we spit in His face, as we are doing now? We need to pray for national revival. May God bless America again and open the heavens to pour down His reign of mercy and healing over our great nation.

What if God is reminding us through this pandemic that if our nation and our lives are built on Him, our foundation will be firm and secure and enable us to weather any storm, while any other foundation we attempt to trust in will turn out to be a sinking sand? What if God is using this crisis to force our political leaders to effectively work together to serve as a reminder, "United, we stand, but divided, we fall." What if God is reminding us during this time of economic stress that He is our source of provision, and everything we have, or ever will have, is, ultimately, from Him?

Maybe God is having us reclassify what jobs are truly essential for our society to function, because the truth is, we were able to get by without March Madness, without the NBA sports, concerts, movies, or theater, but we can't get by without the healthcare professionals, scientists, trash collectors, grocery workers, police officers, military troops, etc. Jesus said for us to love our neighbor as ourselves, but we have not been doing that at all.

What if God allowed churches' doors to close to remind believers and non-believers that the church has never been about a building, but that true spiritual revival comes from a renewed hunger for a real relationship with God through Jesus Christ? Perhaps, God is asking you and I to stop doing life without Him— to stop worrying about tomorrow, but instead, to live in today. Have you seen the tomb, where His body was, and seen it is empty today? Do you know what that means ? It means there's hope, if we allow Him back in America. Not wishful-thinking hope, but sure hope for today and hope for tomorrow: hope for America. The only real hope for all our political dysfunction and all of our hatred and division is a relationship with God.

Any nation that desires to see God move must grasp this truth: we will never see the moving of God collectively in our information-based society until we experience it personally. We have fixated on indicators— weather indicators, economic indicators, and political indicators— even our cars have indicator lights. Amazingly, it was the same in Jesus' day. As we prepare for revival, we need to examine our spiritual condition.

INDICATOR ONE: We decide to deliberately disobey God. However, Jonah knew exactly what God required, but instead of listening, he decided to willfully disobey God, just like we are doing now in America. Obedience is a gentle word for rebellion, and for some reason, we have come to believe that God is willing to bargain with us over His commands. We, as a nation, tend to think that it is reasonable for God to make exceptions to His rules, or at least compromise to some degree. Know this: God does not negotiate His commands. He didn't for Abraham, Moses, nor David, and he will not for us. If we say, "In God we trust," but then qualify it with a, "however…", then we need to return to God.

INDICATOR TWO: We disregard God's correction in the midst of God sending storms. Jonah's deep sleep is a good metaphor for spiritual indifference. Some people today are so "asleep", they completely miss what God is trying to say to them. Is America asleep right now?

INDICATOR THREE: We run from our calling. Jonah got up to flee from the Lord. Is America running from God's calling?

Notice three important phrases here:

"To flee" is the irresponsibility of running from God. When it comes to our calling, our nation can find herself making excuses as to why she can't do it!

"To tarshish" is the insanity of running from God. What is our tarshish as a nation? It is the place we have gone to that is the opposite of God's will for our country. We tried to run as far from God's calling as possible. Obviously, it is not working well for us.

"From God" is the impossibility of running from God. Can America truly escape? Of course not. We can run, but we cannot hide from God. Consider these questions:

1. What has God called America to do?

2. What has God-given us as a passion?

3. When should America do it?

INDICATOR FOUR: We ignore God's Word. It reminds us that God constantly tries to speak to the hearts of His people.

Perhaps we should ask if God has spoken to America's hearts about where we are heading? I believe He has, but the question is: are we listening?

Ultimately, we ignore the word that speaks to our hearts for two reasons:

1. We don't like what God says, nor His commands. Imagine how Jonah felt when he heard the spirit of the Lord say, "Go to Nineveh." He didn't like it at all, just like America is not willing to obey what God wants us to do or commands us not to do .

2. We don't love it as we should. God's Word is truly a love letter, and when we love God, we will want to hear from Him. God is writing a love letter to America, but can we read and accept it and go back to Him before is too late?

So, how do we return back to God? True, discovered grace and forgiveness, plus true, humiliating honesty and confession. We need to start by forgiving one another of all wrongdoings. No matter what your race is, we are one under the umbrella of the Almighty God. Let's ask the

Holy Spirit for His gifts of love peace and joy over each and every one of us in this country. Let's pray for our leaders for wisdom to put us all back together and not divide us. Let's pray for unity and not hate.

Will God bless America again? Can God bless? America, should God bless America? Are we blessable? If God did bless America, what would He be saying about our morality? About our spiritual condition? Could God bless America and protect His reputation as a holy God? Of course, God can always do whatever He wants, whenever He wants, but when it comes to blessings, He has clearly and repeatedly set down conditions. In fact, I think this is a serious intrusion. I don't think we are ready to know the conditions. It's sort of like a, "Don't ask, just bless. Don't ask us to obey you or do right by each other. We just want to be normal again. But God, don't impose any conditions on us. Don't meddle with our immorality."

Frankly, we need to position ourselves to be blessed. Because blessings always have conditions. We just need to go to scripture. If there's ever going to be a blessing, the first thing that has to happen is we have to bring back prayers in our country. We need to completely surrender to the authority of the Almighty God. Israel knew there was no mystery to the standards for blessings. Israel knew that they possessed the eternal covenant and had been given everlasting promises. They knew that God is a faithful God, but they also knew that God could punish them, because He is a holy God.

If God can get so angry with the children of Israel and remove them from His sight, we Americans need to be very careful how we treat God. We need to examine our consciences about how we treat each other. Love is the key to the problems we are facing today. We were created in peace and love, but greed, hatred, and selfishness have overturned everything in the world. Matthew 19:23-24 says, "Then Jesus said to his disciples, 'Truly I tell you; it is hard for someone who is rich to enter the kingdom of heaven. Again, I tell you, it is easier for a camel to go through the eye of a needle than for someone who is rich to enter the kingdom of God.'"

God created all men equal. Each and every person is a perculiar gift of nature to balance life's equation. Everybody was created for a purpose. The devil brought in pride in us, which blinded our visions of being our neighbors' keepers, like the Lord always urges us to be. I always ask people, "Can you be a leader if there is no one to be ruled or lead?" Everybody I have asked said, "No."

This practically means you and I are nobody without each other. The whole world is in chaos, and the younger generations are being led the wrong way. Is there anything wrong if we all help each other be better people? It is time that we come together as a country and forgive each other, because each and every one of us have offended the other side. We need to come together and break this generational curse; we cannot keep carrying it over from generation to generation.

There's this saying: "The house that is free of rats doesn't have to worry about where the roasted fish was kept." So, we can all move this country forward. If we don't show love to one another, we cannot fix it. We have to start by practicing being our brother's keeper and stop hating each other. Without real love, nothing will be solved.

So, I challenge you to show one person you don't know love. I pray that after reading this book, by special grace and mercy, God will bring us back to Him and bring us back to loving one another.

God bless America. Is America an end to greatness or the beginning? Oftentimes, nations strive to make it to the top as world leaders, and when on the top, ego, malice, racial issues, envy, and philosophical differences set into the loving nation to divide and destroy it. Whenever these vices take over a great nation, division ensues. President Ronald Regan brought peace to America when he ended the bitter Cold War with the Soviet Union. Most of the countries that have risen to the top will always start their rapid discent due to division within,

followed by natural disasters or pandemics, and the next potential world leaders will capitalize on their internal crises to emerge as the new world leader.

America's greatness was attained in the 80s, when president Ronald Regan—a non-politically oriented president— received the flag of greatness from the great Soviet Union after he bluffed his way to ending the Cold War. Can the political elites ever get things done fast, without trying to be politically correct? President Ronald Regan accomplished more for America and the world by not being politically and legally correct all the time. America, just like other great nations of the past, attained greatness only to divide and self-destruct down the line. How can we forget the great Egyptian state, the Roman empire, the great British regime, or the great Mali empire in Africa?

It is always difficult for a divided nation to withstand any external aggression or major natural disasters, like what America is going through now, without the invocation of the great, American spirits to quickly unite this great nation. Her days as the global leader might soon be over. The next potential leader of this world might be popping champagne in wait for the rare opportunity to lead. Who might that be? China? North Korea? Russia? My fellow Christians should remember the story of how the church conspired against Jesus Christ to be crucified, because he changed the ways churches were seeing and doing things. America is the only country in the world that never trusted her government, nor its leaders, but firmly and deeply professed the unequivocal trust in God by dedicating her currency back to God. Take a look at our dollar bill, and see for yourself. The founders of this great nation firmly believed in God, and it should remain a God-loving nation.

I wonder what the forefathers of this great nation are doing in their graves now, after seeing the increase in moral decadences and the escalating political division. Let all of us unite together and save this great nation. God bless America.